SURVIVING THE INTERNET

A Guide for Parents and Kids

by

Lawrence G Fine

Table of Contents

Foreword

Who should read this book

There have been several books and articles written on the topic of internet safety. They include resources for parents, teachers, and responsible website owners to help keep young people safe on the internet. But there has never been a book written just for you. There has never been a book teaching young people how to keep themselves safe, resources for them to use.

This book is written with one goal in mind. That is, to keep you safe on the internet; to keep you from becoming the latest "Breaking News" story, or the latest "Amber Alert". Everyone knows about the dangers in general, whether it be identity theft, stalking, or getting lured into a bad situation. But few people really sit down and calculate the risks involved with giving out or using the information on the internet.

How often in your daily life do you really stop before you enter your email address on a website, and think "I wonder where this goes?" How often do you do a background check on people you are chatting with? Most people know all of this information, and yet don't put it into practice on a daily basis. It is like knowing where the bad neighborhoods are, but preferring to risk walking alone at night wherever is most convenient.

That is why this book was written. To protect

you, to protect your family, and to protect those you know from the dangers of the World Wide Web. To make you aware of the real risks involved in activities most of us participate in without even thinking. To save you from learning the dangers first hand. Once reading this book, you should know what to avoid and how to avoid it. Most importantly, you should know what to do if you or a friend becomes an internet victim.

There are two primary reasons that you should be reading this book. Your main reason for reading is undoubtedly so that you are aware of the dangers and risks involved with activity on the internet, and how to avoid becoming a victim yourself. But, you should also read this book so that you can spot the danger signs that friends and family may show when participating in these activities.

Throughout this book, along with tips to avoid becoming a victim, the warning signs of a potential victim will be described. If you or someone you know is exhibiting these signs, you need to tell a responsible adult right away. It doesn't have to be a parent, a teacher, or even a counselor. It can even be an older sibling. The most important thing is that the adult you trust can take the action required to protect you. If this book can make just one person aware of these risks, it really can make a difference.

This book contains the term "internet crime" more than once, and there is a very specific reason for this. Most of the dangerous activities warned about in this book are actually illegal to participate in.

Those who commit these "internet crimes" can be subject to punishment by law, consisting of fines, a criminal record, house arrest, and even jail time. It is important to remember that victims of internet crimes are just that, victims. Just like the victims of other crimes, they often go unheard. Don't be a statistic. If you or someone you know is a victim of an internet crime, tell someone! Some of us may remember our parents telling us, "It isn't you I don't trust, it's everyone else." And that is especially true of the internet. When you are online, if you become the victim of an internet crime, you are not at fault, and you are not a criminal. You are a victim, and you have rights.

There are a few important resources that must be noted here. If you become the victim of an internet crime, and you don't feel comfortable telling your parents or teachers, there are other people who can help you. Your school counselors may be able to offer some help, and even some counseling. If your school has a Police Liaison Officer, talk with them about internet safety. Some schools even have a student council dedicated to internet safety that you can talk to about your problems. If your school doesn't have one, talk to your principal about starting this group. You could be more helpful than you realize.

Go on reading remembering one thing. Although this book warns of the most common dangers on the internet, it couldn't possibly contain them all. Use your common sense, and don't do anything if it doesn't feel right. You are a member of the most advanced society man-kind has ever created. You have infinite resources available at your disposal. Remember that with great power comes great responsibility, and you have a responsibility to be a law abiding and careful internet user. If you take this responsibility seriously, the internet will be a safer place for everyone.

Happy reading, and stay safe.

PART 1

The Truth – Fact Or Fiction?

The reliability of information on the internet

The mis-information super highway

Who could have imagined five or ten years ago how much the internet would become a part of our daily lives. The encyclopedia is now a website, the card catalog is a search engine, and telephone conversations have all but been replaced with instant messengers. The library, while still a good source for information, is no longer the first resource of choice for many of us. With the vast array of information available at our fingertips, 24 hours a day 7 days a week, you have the incredible power to find out in seconds what would have taken hours of research before. However, with this great power comes a great responsibility.

With this fountain of information available to us, it has become our responsibility to distinguish the truth from fiction. The internet is full of information, and not all of it is as reliable as some would have you believe. You don't have to look very far to find fiction masquerading as fact, or vice versa. In fact, look no farther than your favorite search engine. But it can be very difficult to tell fact and fiction apart in some cases. This first chapter is all about the answers to, and the risks of, this significant problem.

Once upon a time, when our parents were writing papers for science class or social studies, they had printed resources. One of the benefits of these resources is that they were screened. People hand-picked these resources, verified their reliability, and put their stamp of approval on them. The library essentially had two sections; One fact, the other fiction. They were very distinguishable, and very easy to tell apart.

Now, the lines between fact and fiction are not nearly as clear-cut as they were. There is no "fact" section on the internet. No one is there to read every website, and make sure that the content is reliable. Websites aren't "hand-picked" to be allowed on the internet. It is up to us to decide whether what we are reading is the truth.

Misinformation takes many forms. Sometimes it may not seem like fiction. Many websites present their information in an "article" format, similar to that in a newspaper. Sometimes it may appear to be far from the truth, when it is in fact based on sound reasoning and is a verifiable fact. Other times it may appear to be a perfect reference for a homework assignment, when in reality it is a collection of made-up facts.

There are several types of misleading websites on the internet. One example would be the "hate site". For everyone who loves a product, theory, or idea, there is someone opposed to it. These sites are very easy to distinguish, as often you will only see negative content about the subject. There may be the occasional defense, in the case of a public forum, but the majority of the content will reflect negatively on the subject. If everything on the website appears to be negative in nature, and contains mostly general comments, chances are that you are viewing a "hate site".

Just the opposite of "hate sites", "fan sites" are websites that are overly optimistic or positive about the subject. Many celebrity fan sites are personal websites, designed and developed by one individual or group to simply share their praise for a certain celebrity. More often than not, however, fan sites are simply websites designed by businesses to promote their products or services. Just like with hate sites, if everything on the website is overly positive, you are most likely viewing a fan site.

Another example of a misleading website would be a commercial website. Many of these are simply advertisements disguised as valuable content. These sites are actually easier to be fooled by, because some companies spend millions of dollars researching how to make the website work best on consumers like you. These are similar to fan sites, but have some similarities to hate sites as well. Often, with a commercial website, you will see a lot of positive information about the product (either specific, like brand names, or in general, like "candy is good", etc.) followed by a lot of negative information about the alternatives (yet again, either specific of general. i.e. "fruit is bad.")

One type of misleading website has actually been around in some form long before the existence of the internet. There are so many of these websites on the world wide web now that it is getting harder to believe any health information found on the internet. Scammers have a huge advantage now with the internet, in that they have a new and more efficient way of reaching their targets. The main thing to remember about sites like this is that if it sounds too good to be true, then it probably is. Nothing that is worth your time can be sped up with money.

Personal opinions are another common type of misinformation site. After all, the internet is essentially a network of people sharing information. When people share information, it is usually biased in some way towards their own personal opinions. Most personal opinion websites are individuals' personal websites, where they post information that they believe or want others to believe. More recently, the advent of blogs has made it even easier to find personal opinion sites on the internet. Blogging has made it easy for anyone who can send an email to have their voice heard, even if their voice isn't the most reliable source for information.

Parody or spoof sites are another common category of misleading websites. Typically a search for any current events will bring up several spoof or parody websites, mocking either the subject of the current event or the individuals involved. These websites are intentionally misleading, although not intended to be harmful. Usually parody or spoof sites are created either for fun as a joke, or to make a political point about a current event. Occasionally, however, parody or spoof sites are created simply to prove how easy it is to fool someone on the internet.

The final category of misleading information is the email hoax. Every one of us has received an email hoax, except maybe for those of us living under a rock. These are often chain letters, forwarded from one friend to another. They often consist of urban legends, false virus or health warnings, or scams about making easy money. These are particularly easy to spot, because they usually have some kind of ridiculous claim attached to them. Once again, if it sounds too good to be true, it probably is.

The risks of using the information from these sites vary in severity, but they all do carry risks. If used for homework, you can fail your assignment or even the whole class. If used to make important decisions, you could make the wrong decision, and anything could happen. It is important to take information you find on the internet in context, and as your mother always said, "consider the source."

There are few warning signs that someone is being led on by misleading information, other than the obvious act of telling you something that you know isn't true. But there are some things to watch out for. For example, if your friend seems uncontrollably excited about something they read on the internet, but are incredibly secretive, they may be the victim of an email hoax. Often after a few days, your friend will no longer be interested in discussing their internet secret. This is a good sign, because it means they have discovered that it was a hoax.

Remember not to be discouraged about

information on the internet. There are ways to safeguard against misinformation. First, always double check your sources. Once you find the fact you are looking for, go to your favorite encyclopedia site (such as Britannica.com) and double check the information. Check if your source is credible. Do they post contact details online? Do they have a disclaimer on their website about their information? Are you using an online encyclopedia, or someone's personal website? Can you verify the information you've found using the information on other websites? When was this website last updated? Is there a place other than the internet you can use to confirm this information? All of these are important questions to ask when using information found on the internet, as they can save you from tremendous amounts of hassle.

Misinformation on the internet is no joke, it is a real problem. If it isn't recognized early, there can be serious consequences to using the information. Be careful when researching on the internet, and if you get discouraged, remember that there is always the public library. Use your judgment, and always double check your sources elsewhere. You will save yourself a lot of time and headache.

Phish Tales

When good people let bad things happen.

Phishing is a serious problem

Identity theft isn't just an adult problem. Even you can become a victim if you aren't careful. Phishing is when a spammer or other online con-artist pretends that they are your bank, insurance company, or another company with access to your sensitive information. They will often do a very good job of copying graphics, links, and stationary to appear to be "the real thing". The email will then ask you to verify your password, your account number, or some other information that normally the bank would have.

A word of caution; Never, EVER click on the link in that email. If you get an email that you believe may be from your bank or another institution, go directly to their website (the way you normally access it), and report the email. They will usually reply within minutes telling you if the email is a fake or not. Most of the time these emails are false. Remember that your bank or other institution already has this information. They do not need you to confirm it in an email. Also, it may give you tips for protection against these emails right on the website of these companies. Remember that if information is needed from you, your bank or insurance company would never request it through email.

You may be able to tell if you are a target for

phishing simply by checking your email. If you start to notice a lot of email from companies you don't deal with, asking to confirm your information, chances are that you are on a mailing list for these scammers. Oftentimes you will even get scam emails from companies that don't exist, such as "Trusted Bank" or "Insurance Inc."

Phishing is a real problem today. In October 2009, over 350 brands have been reported to have been hijacked by phishing campaigns, 74% of these phishing scams were done through e-mail. Phishers will often use URLs that look like the appropriate address, but add just enough to redirect you to their phishing site. An example might be www.trustedbank.fake.com. This URL is obviously false, but many phishers will use letters or numbers in place of the word "fake" to look like technical information that you see in many URLs. There are some phishing sites that have resorted to using IP addresses instead of the URL to further confuse the victims. Some phishers have even gone as far as hacking into legitimate websites and stealing your information if you visit while they have access.

Phishing isn't just limited to email, either. Phishing attacks on users of social networking sites go back to the very early days of the crime, when scammers would attempt to steal AOL passwords using chat rooms and instant messengers. Some experiments have shown a success rate of over 70% for phishing attacks on social networking sites like Facebook; a whopping seven out of ten users who are presented with a phishing scam will enter their information.

The damage caused by phishing is far reaching, and can destroy lives. It can ruin credit, destroy social relationships and leave individuals with trust issues. But there are ways that you can fight back against phishing scams. The easiest way involves simply continuing what you are doing right now, and educating yourself on the signs of phishing scams and the risks involved. You can also watch for signs in your email that what you are viewing may be a phishing scam. Often, email from legitimate companies will contain some kind of personalization; Whether it be your real name, your username, or even a partial account number. Emails with greetings such as "Dear _____ Customer" or "Valued Customers" should be viewed as suspicious. Make sure you have the latest technology installed on your computer to help protect you from phishing. Some newer versions of web browsers actually include a warning that tells you when you visit a potential phishing site. Other new email programs include a warning when you are viewing an email that may be a phishing scam. Don't rely only on these measures, however. A software program is no replacement for common sense.

Hey, I Know You!

Your identity and the internet

You're more popular than you think
Identity theft isn't just an adult problem. Even you can become a victim if you aren't careful. Your identity, especially today, is a valuable item. It is something that no one else has, and that those with ill intentions desire. Treat your identity like a valuable gem. Never show it to anyone, never tell anyone about it, and keep it under lock and key. The more you boast about your identity, the more thieves will want it. You wouldn't go around the internet posting pictures and locations of a precious diamond, don't do it with your identity.

There are a lot more people out there than you think who want your information. Everyone has heard about the problems with identity theft. There are credit cards being forged, bank accounts being hijacked, and peoples' lives being destroyed. But your identity isn't just about your sensitive financial information. Even the youngest internet surfers can be victims of privacy invasions.

There are many ways to get your information using the internet. It only takes one form, one email, one chat room message for your identity to become a fraudster's playground. Things to beware of include filling out surveys & contest entry forms, registering for internet services like email, instant messengers and file-sharing programs, completing a personal

10

profile for your email or instant messenger account, creating a profile on a social networking site like Facebook or Twitter, or giving information, even just your name or phone number, to people in chat rooms and over instant messenger.

If you do any of these things, chances are that your information is scattered all over the World Wide Web for everyone to see. If you have an account in any social networking site, chances are, people will find you and target you. It would start simple enough: a message exchange over similar interests that can lead to you adding each other up as contacts. More questions will follow: "What is your dog's name?" or "What school do you go to?" Unfortunately, the answers to these questions are often also the answers to the users' "secret questions", allowing hackers to change the users' passwords and gain full access to their account.

The information you enter in forms online can also be used against you in legal ways. Companies will often purchase the information in bulk, with the intentions of using the information for marketing purposes. In marketing circles, this is known as "co-registration". Essentially, this means that when you sign up to one website, you are signing up to the other website as well, giving the marketer full access to the information in the forms. This information can be used against you, like when a company wants to market their new product to you. They know exactly what you like, where you live, and who you hang out with. This makes it very easy for them to influence you into purchasing without you even knowing it.

That's why it's important to thoroughly read the fine print when you sign up for a website or an online service. Oftentimes, forms would have pre-checked items, so be sure to double check what you are signing up for.

There are a lot more risks than marketing messages when you give your information out over the internet. Cyber-stalking, online bullying and even identity theft can happen. Remember, just because you aren't an adult now doesn't mean you never will be. Someone could use your information and pretend to be you. If they know your age and your birthday, it will be easy for them to know when they can really do damage to your life. Young people with criminal records who are looking to cross borders will often seek the identity information of someone of a similar age who is similar in appearance. You make have the exact likeness of a fugitive, and not even know it. The problem appears when they know it. They will use your identity to cross borders, sign documents, and commit crimes. You could end up with a criminal record because of a young identity thief.

One of the most over-looked ways of protecting your information is actually in front of you every day. For every website on which you use any personal information, read their privacy policy. Most are fairly standard issue, but some are not. These privacy policies are legal documents that companies have spent hundreds, or even thousands of dollars to write up to protect them. The problem is that they don't protect you. There have been cases where the company's privacy policy actually said that they would sell your information, use it for market research, and gather information on your surfing habits. That information is on the website for a reason. When you click agree, you are legally saying "okay" to whatever they just wrote. You wouldn't sign a contract for a job or a purchase without reading it, so why agree to a privacy policy without reading it first? Spending an extra five minutes can save you a lifetime of trouble.

Any information is dangerous

It is obvious that personal information includes things such as your Social Security Number, legal name, address and so forth. But how much information really is personal information. Take, for example, your phone number. You have probably given it to more than one online friend. But, using just your phone number, your online friend could easily find out where you live, what your last name is, who your parents are, and even figure out what school you go to. Giving your phone number to the wrong person is very, very dangerous. If an online predator had your phone number, and got all of the information above, they could very easily come to your school, have you called to the office, and kidnap you right there. Any information is dangerous in the hands of the wrong people.

There are many ways to avoid becoming a victim of identity theft. The most important thing is to always know who you are giving your important information to. Even when you know who is on the receiving end of your information, you should always be sure that you are sending the information over a secure connection. Instant messengers and private messages in chat rooms are not secure. Just because it appears that no one else is watching doesn't make that true. You could have key-logging software installed on your computer and not even know it. You type in something that looks like a credit card number, the key-logger records it, and sends it to an online scam artist. Presto, you are a victim of identity theft.

With all the ways to avoid identity security issues, identity theft can still happen. It is important to recognize the warning signs in your friends and family so that you can help them if they ever become a victim of identity crimes.

Warning signs of identity theft include receiving bills for accounts you didn't open, seeing unauthorized charges on your cell phone bill, bank account or credit card, being contacted by a collection agency for a debt you didn't incur, your bills arriving late suddenly when they have always been on time, or mail disappearing all together.

You should also watch for signs that could indicate one of your friends participating in identity crimes. Addicts, whether they are drug abusers, alcoholics or gamblers, all have a need for cash and a taste of crime. Watch out for friends living well beyond their means. If your friend works at a fast food restaurant and filed for bankruptcy six months ago suddenly drives up in a luxury SUV, be suspicious. Make sure to change passwords and security information after break-ups or bad fights with friends or boyfriends/girlfriends. Often they have both the means and the motive to wreak havoc on your identity.

The Internet Persona

The new identity crisis

So-called freedom

The internet isn't like your parents' house or your school's lunch room. There aren't people watching out for you every moment of the day. You don't spend every waking minute with people who know you in and out. It is very easy to say and do whatever you want, or even be whomever you want, when you are on the world wide web.

Many young adults like you think that it is easier to get away with things on the internet. No one can track them down, they are online. Hurting other people on the internet is easy, because you can just hide behind your email address, right? Wrong. An email address, while a marvel of technology, can't simply "hide you" and where you are located. Take a look at the headers in an email, and you will see. They will often include what is called an IP address (IP stands for Internet Protocol). This address can uniquely identify who your internet service provider is, and in turn identify who you are, all with this unique little number.

You cannot hide behind the internet and use it for ill purposes. Many court cases in the United States and around the world have been won because the person who committed a crime used the internet, and therefore their IP address was logged and tracked down. Enforcement agencies such as the FBI, CIA and even local and regional police services have the capability to track down individuals based solely on their IP address. And if, hypothetically speaking, a certain police or enforcement organization were to find themselves unable to track down an individual, they could simply contact the suspected Internet Service Provider (or ISP) and have them tracked down that way.

You shouldn't fear this technology, but rather be glad it exists. It is because of IP tracking technology that you can feel a little bit safer on the internet. If an individual commits a crime on the internet, they can and will be caught, most likely because of IP tracking technology.

Some individuals feel that they are invincible on the internet, because of the anonymity. As you can see from the information above, this is just not true. There is no anonymity on the internet. Every website you visit, every email you send, every activity you participate in (even chat rooms) can all be tracked with your IP address. Remember this the next time you or someone you know thinks of acting out online, because they are "anonymous". To put it simply, you are not anonymous, but instead easily traceable. And if you choose to break laws or violate the rights of others on the internet, you will be caught; Just as others will if they choose to do the same.

Cyber Bullies

Taking the school ground to a new level

Cyber bullies are, quite simply, people who bully others over the internet. They may send their messages using email, text messages, instant messenger, chat rooms, blogs, or even building entire websites designed to insult or threaten someone. Based on a study made in 2007, 32% of teens have experienced being harassed online. Most of these teens are aged between 14 and 17 years old, a majority of them girls.

Unfortunately, cyber bullying usually goes farther than name calling. Cyber bullies are rude and mean to others on the internet because they feel they cannot be caught. If they can't be caught, they can do whatever they want. This creates a dangerous environment, where violence and hate run free.

Some examples of cyber bullying you might see include threats, gossip, hate mail, and even entire websites dedicated to blackmailing people. What makes cyber bullying even more dangerous is that it is often unseen by adults. Normally, when someone gets bullied, a teacher or a parent will notice and intervene before things get out of hand. However, if the bullying is limited to instant messages, email, text messages and forum posts, parents and other responsible adults likely will not have access to them. It won't even be obvious what is happening until too late. You make take it for granted, but having responsible adults around to intervene is very important. It prevents things from escalating to a level that you and everyone else your age simply cannot handle alone.

There are some very simple ways to avoid cyber bullies. First, ignore them! Remember that the best thing about the internet is that YOU control what you want to see and read. If you don't want to see or read something a cyber bully is saying to you, ignore them. Cyber bullies enjoy this activity because they get a reaction from people. If you don't give a reaction, they won't have a reason to bother you. The "close" button works wonders for this.

There are warning signs that friends or parents may be the victim of cyber bullying. Watch for these signs, and if you suspect they are being victimized, get help for them immediately! Often victims of cyber bullying will be unwilling or even afraid to seek help themselves. The only way to help them is to get help for them.

Cyber bullying is actually one of the easiest of internet crimes to detect. Victims of cyber bullying may spend long hours on their computer, close windows or shut off the monitor when you come in the room, be secretive about their online activities, suddenly change their behavior, may get mysterious telephone calls during the day or late at night, fear of leaving the house, crying for no obvious reason, low self esteem, unexplained broken or lost possessions or money, and excuses that don't seem to make sense. Essentially, these signs all show feelings of helplessness, fear, suspicion and emotional pain.

If cyber bullying ever begins to involve threats to yourself or others, or to any property, you need to tell a responsible adult right away. Eventually they will find out, and surely you would rather have their help now than have them find out after something bad has happened. Remember, adults aren't there to make you look "geeky", or to "embarrass" you, or to get angry at you. They are there to protect you and keep you as safe as possible. All you have to do is be a responsible young adult and tell them when you need their help.

It goes the other way too
Cyberbullying, while mostly perpetrated by minors to fellow minors, are done by teens to adults as well. Ever wrote a rant about a teacher who failed you or posted an incriminating photo? That is cyberbullying as well.

There have been a rise in cases of teachers in particular, who have experienced being bullied. Most of these attacks were done online. In a study made in 2009, 63% of the respondents were attacked via e-mail, while 26% had offensive posts written about them in social networking sites. There were also cases wherein the students who wrote these posts have been suspended from school, and had it marked in their permanent records.

While it is understandable to rant and vent out your frustration, remember that words are powerful. They can do as much damage as they can do wonders for you and the people around you.

Adult Content

The birds and the bees, internet style

Pornography

We all see it. It is all over the internet. It is hard to avoid, and often accidental. It is pornography. It makes up 12% of all websites on the internet, 8% of all emails, 35% of all downloads, and 25% of all search engine requests. The average age of first exposure to internet pornography is 11 years old. Eleven! It is easy to see why. The adult industry is worth $97 billion each year to the world's economy. That's $97,000,000,000.00; more than the combined annual revenue of all professional baseball, basketball, football and hockey franchises in North America. That is a large incentive to get internet users hooked, and hooked young.

There are risks involved, such as suspension from school or contracting viruses and Trojans on your computer. However, the most important thing to know about adult content on the internet is what to do when it happens to you.

Statistics show that almost one fifth of all young people accidentally end up on an adult website within a one year period. These aren't the ones who just "say" it was an accident; these are real kids who accidentally stumbled onto the wrong website. It is actually very easy to do. Adult website managers often employ tricky tactics to get users onto their websites. An adult site web master may find a way to install a script on your computer that changes your home page to their website. Changing it back will appear to work, but once you reboot your computer, the site is back again. Some adult websites earn money for every website view they have. They make agreements with other websites to show a "pop-up" or "pop-under" window when you visit the other company's website. Often times there will be a built-in script with the window that causes hundreds of other windows to open every time you close one. Some adult sites purposely mask themselves as other websites. They will often buy up old URLs that once pointed to more friendly content in an attempt to get more traffic to their website. Some websites will even bury certain keywords, like the names of popular toys, in the coding of their website where search engines can find it. Anyone searching for that particular toy can end up at an adult website.

You should also know the warning signs to recognize if a friend or family member is viewing adult content. Remember that viewing these websites intentionally while under the age of majority is a crime. You can help prevent internet crimes by watching for warning signs like friends spending large amounts of time at the computer, clearing the internet history every time they go online, closing windows when you walk in the room, or muting the volume on their computer all the time.

The important thing to know here is that some adult website owners make it very easy for you to accidentally end up on their website. If you happen to end up there by accident, don't just sit and worry that you will get caught. Be proactive, and go tell a responsible adult what happened right away. Chances are, if you go and tell them that you just accidentally ended up at an adult website and didn't know what to do, they will thank you for being honest and help you to avoid it in the future.

Sex, Drugs, And Parental Controls?

Why information on these topics is less than reliable.

Would you let him do your homework?

Imagine, for a moment, what you picture a "drug user" or "drug addict" to look like. Do you picture a highly intelligent, well presented individual? Or someone who has more fingers than brain cells? If nothing else, you most likely didn't choose the first possibility. Many of the individuals in society who participate in these activities also end up with mental and/or intellectual challenges as a result of their addiction.

Now, think for a moment of someone at school you know who uses drugs. You may not know them personally, but they are in every school. We have all met them, and they are the "Stoners". Imagine you had an important assignment coming due in a week. This homework assignment would mean the difference between an "A+" or a fail in the class, depending on how well you did. It is a sink or swim assignment. Would you ask one of "The Stoners" to do it for you? Would you trust their intelligence and information to pass that class? Or would you do it yourself, knowing you could do better?

Your answer above is very important. If you wouldn't let a stoner write an assignment for school, why would you trust them with your life? Illegal drugs are no joke. Marijuana, ecstasy, methamphetamines, cocaine, heroin and countless other drugs kill thousands of people each and every year. They can be extremely dangerous, and even the tiniest amounts can be lethal. Why would you trust your life to a drug addict?

If you ever think of reading information on drugs from the internet, consider this. Who are the people who know so much about drugs? Who are the people who are willing to share it? Who are the people who have access to this kind of information whenever they want it? Drug addicts do. If you are reading information on the internet about "how to buy drugs" or "how to make drugs" or "getting high at home", you are most likely reading something that was written by a drug addict. Knowing that drugs like these are potentially lethal, and knowing that you wouldn't even trust a simple homework assignment to a stoner, why on earth would you trust them with your life?

You are an intelligent young adult, and you can make the right decisions. It may sound cliché, but you are the future of this world. Without you, there is no future. A world without you is a world without hope. You deserve to live a long and happy life, and the world deserves to have you. Use your head, don't do drugs, and don't rely on the internet to teach you about them. Instead, sit down and talk to your parents.

It may feel uncomfortable at first, but really your parents want you to talk to them about things like this. They have already been through what you are going through; All the peer pressure, the media glorification, everything you are seeing about drugs they have already seen. Your parents are the one group of people on earth who will be honest with you about drugs. They won't talk to you like a child, they won't just say "don't do drugs", like so many after-school specials. Your parents will tell you the truth, answer your questions, and help you through this time. Use that resource to your full advantage.

Sex information on the internet
One day while surfing the internet, you might find yourself curious about sex. That is a normal part of being a young adult. Sex is something that you are bombarded with each and every day, and yet you likely haven't had any experience with it. It is natural to be curious. But the internet is not the best resource to learn about sex.

Think for a minute about the information you find on the internet about sex. First, you will likely find a lot of pornography. You may even stumble onto illegal websites. This is not the way to go. There are three resources that can help you to find information about sex. One is this book; Another, your school; And of course, your parents can help teach you about sex.

It may seem uncomfortable to talk to your parents about sex, but remember this. Your parents once had "the talk" with their parents, and their parents had "the talk" with their parents. "The talk" is something that every young adult experiences at one point or another. Remember also that your parents now have more information at their fingertips than ever before. They are encouraged by the media, the schools, and other parents to talk to you about sex. They know how to do it right, with as little "uncomfortable silence" as possible. If you have questions about sex, your parents should be your first resource.

Your school also has several resources available to them to help with your quest for information. Years ago, sex education in schools only taught abstinence. Nowadays, schools teach young adults everything they need to know about sex. From the "mechanics" of the birds and the bees, to Sexually Transmitted Diseases, to pregnancy and beyond. Schools have learned that the "just don't do it" approach doesn't work with intelligent young adults today. So they give reasons why you should abstain from sex, as well as how to be safe if you do engage in those activities. Your school likely has a sexual education teacher, or a counselor who specializes in that information. If you have questions, you can also ask them.

If you are determined to find information about sexuality and your sexual health using the internet, there are ways to find this information while still staying safe. The most important thing is to tell your parents what you are doing. They will likely help point you in the right directions, and you are less likely to get in trouble for visiting those kinds of websites. For starters, you should avoid just typing "sex" into your search engine. The websites that pop up will not be the ones you are looking for. Try visiting sites like www.HowStuffWorks.com, www.Wikipedia.org, or www.KidsHealth.org. These are all websites that are designed to teach you, rather than sell you pornographic material. Ask your parents to direct you to some websites, or ask your school counselor if they have any websites to suggest. The best way to find information about your sexuality online is to ask someone offline to point you in the right direction. Even your local librarian might be able to help.

The Band-Aid Solution

Today it is becoming easier and easier to find software on the internet that claims to protect you from internet crime and websites you, as a young adult, shouldn't be viewing. Do a search engine search for "parental controls", and you will find millions of results. While much of this software is effective in some ways, no one parental control can protect you completely. In fact, they may just be giving you a false sense of security.

Parental controls work by blocking certain kinds of websites on the internet. When you type in a URL in your web browser, the parental control will search the text of the web page. If they find words that may not be suitable for you to view, they will block the web page. However, this is not a catch-all solution. Many websites may not have the right words to trigger a parental control, but still have content that isn't suitable for you to view. Other resources, like chat rooms and instant messengers, are not blocked. This leaves a lot to be desired when it comes to filtering the content you have available to you on the internet.

There are solutions that will do almost the opposite of a typical parental control, and only allow you to view websites that your parents have already approved. The problem with this solution is that it takes a lot of time to set up, and if you find a new website you would like to view – even if it is "ColoringBook.com" or something similar, your parents have to manually review and approve it.

As you can see, there is no one solution that can protect you on the internet completely. However, using a combination of parental controls and your own intelligence, you can stay safe on the internet. While it may seem that parental controls are only there to restrict what you can do on the internet, it is important to remember that they are there for your own personal safety.

If you or your parents are looking for a good software solution, there are a few things to look for. First, you should be able to block websites on demand. You should be able to filter specific content from being viewed, and take screen-shots of that content if necessary. The software should automatically record all instant messages, emails, websites, and keystrokes on the computer, and should be accessible from anywhere over the internet, allowing your parents to monitor your activities while they are at work.

One solution has been found that is very highly recommended. It is called WebWatcher, and is available from AwarenessTech at

AwarenessTech.com. It has won several awards, including several "Editor's Choice" awards, and has been featured on CNN and CBS, as well as in publications offered by Newsweek and CNet. As well as having all of the recommended features above, it can also monitor several computers at once, monitors in real-time, is completely invisible on the computers that have it installed, it cannot be stopped by anti-spyware, anti-virus or firewall software, and can even monitor different users on the same computer (so you can see who is doing the viewing).

Just remember that using this or any other software will not guarantee your safety on the internet. While it may help protect you, the only thing that can really protect you is your own common sense.

Online Predators

Who is really watching?

An online predator is essentially an online stalker. They may follow you around online, chat with you constantly, send you disturbing photographs, and insist on meeting with you in person. Online predators are probably the most well known danger on the internet, and they are also the most dangerous. There are several things you should know about online predators, and the way they act.

First, online predators will establish themselves as "one of the group". This means pretending to be just another young adult in the chat room or forum. Predators will typically assume the identity of a teenage girl, because they feel teenage girls connect more easily with other teenage girls. An online predator will introduce themselves, listen to your problems, and try to seem like a really great friend. They will slowly begin to introduce mature content into your conversations, as a way of testing the waters. They may even show you pictures or videos of an adult nature. Many predators will use this time to evaluate the possibility of their "prey" meeting them face-to-face. Younger teens are especially at risk. Online predators see them as vulnerable and naive, making them prime targets.

Predators will often take their time luring in their prey, often sending them gifts through the mail and giving them private email accounts and phone numbers to make contact with. Some predators will even register a toll-free number, so that long distance charges won't "tip off" your parents to the crime.

Online predators are stalkers. They are committing harassment, and harassment is a crime punishable by law. If you are a victim of an online predator, you are a victim of harassment. You have the right to justice, and you should seek that justice starting with your local police force. Police take these kinds of complaints very seriously, because they know what can happen if they don't.

There are many ways to avoid this situation all together. Primarily, be responsible in your online activities. Don't use un-moderated chat rooms, as predators will usually hang out there. Moderated chat rooms have the ability to "kick" a user out if they begin disrupting the group and making individuals uncomfortable.

Try to avoid "PMs", or private messages, unless it is someone you have met in person. Using a moderated chat room means nothing in private chat, because no one can monitor what happens there. It is the same as meeting new people in person. You always want to meet in a public place for safety. Online, make sure you meet everyone in a public area. It really will keep you safe.

Don't respond to "PMs" from people you don't know. Often they will seem nice, but as soon as you reply they know they have found their target. It is important to have someone to watch over your interactions with new people for your own safety.

If you ever agree to meet face-to-face with an online friend, there are several things you should do. First, tell a responsible adult where you will be and what you are doing. Ask your parents if they feel it is okay. Second, be sure to meet somewhere that is very public, like the library or coffee shop. Third, and most important, never go alone. Always have at least two friends with you when you meet an online "friend". That way, if they do turn out to be a predator, they will be less likely to attempt to hurt you with someone who is watching you.

It is very important in today's society to watch out for your friends and family. There are specific warning signs associated with victims of cyber stalking, and they should be taken seriously. Often a victim will spend large amounts of time on the computer. They may have pornographic images stored in their "received files" folder. They may send or receive phone calls from people you don't know. Often, victims will receive gifts in the mail, and may become withdrawn from family and friends. This is because a common tactic of online predators is to turn the victim against their family and friends to reduce the risk of the victim reporting the crime.

The most important thing to know about staying safe from online predators is to be responsible, and never be afraid of telling someone you trust. Remember, if an online predator tries to take advantage of you, YOU are the victim. Tell a responsible adult whom you trust. They will be glad you came to them before anything happened.

Social networking and cyberstalking
Today's technology has made it easier to share information with our friends and family. Unfortunately, it has also made it easier for stalkers to find you.

There has been a rise in the usage of internet in mobile devices. This means you can update your Facebook or Twitter whereever you are. This also spurred the developing of new social networking sites like FourSquare, which lets you "check in" when you enter a building. This message is broadcasted to your contacts on FourSquare, and if integrated with Twitter and Facebook, will be broadcasted there as well. Just a quick Google search (or a search on Google Maps), people can easily locate you, whether you mean to or not.

Spam

Not just for sandwiches anymore.

Unsolicited commercial email

Unsolicited commercial email, otherwise known as spam, is a large problem on the internet. Some studies have shown that as much as 92% of e-mails received are spam. This translates to more than 2 million spam sent daily. Although it may be a nuisance, spammers (as they are called) don't just send out this email to annoy. They send out these emails to profit. Approximately 1 in 20 individuals who receive a spam message will reply to it or click the link contained within the message. Even legitimate marketers have a hard time getting that many people to read their email.

The other risks

Unfortunately, email isn't the only way to receive spam. Spam can also be sent by instant messenger, through chat rooms, on forums, blogs or social networking sites, and even in search engines. Spammers will go to great lengths to devise new ways of deceiving people out of their money. If a spammer spends five hours researching a new spam tactic, and then sends out a spam that brings them $1000, they are making $200 an hour. That is a large incentive to innovate in this underground industry.

Spam isn't only scamming individuals out of their money. It is also a growing cause of virus and Trojan infection on computers. While anti-spam software can catch most spam email, it can't possibly catch it all. Often the email that does get through the filters contains harmful viruses that can attack your computer and steal your personal information. The only real way of stopping problems like these on your computer is never to open email from someone you don't know.

Tips for preventing spam

There are ways to prevent spam and the risks associated with it. First and most importantly, protect your email address. Posting your email address in a chat room, on a website, or giving it away when signing up for a website are three easy ways to get your email address into the hands of spammers. Look at everything you receive in your inbox with doubt and skepticism. If it sounds too good to be true, it probably is.

You can also protect the e-mail addresses of your friends and family by using the BCC (blind carbon copy) field instead of the To: field in your e-mail client. This way, only their e-mail address appears in the e-mail you sent. This way, even if they forward the e-mail you sent, only your e-mail and their e-mail address will show in the forwarded message. Of course, it's best if you ask them to remove your e-mail address if they will forward, and encourage them to BCC as well.

Double check "urban legend" type email. This is one of the easiest things to do. If you get a "warning" email about a certain product causing harm or catching fire, chances are you are receiving a hoax. Just to be sure, double check the information on the internet. There are entire websites dedicated to revealing these warnings as false. Try www.Snopes.com to double check your information. You can also create a separate email address for "signing up". This way, when you have to enter your email address to access certain websites or content, you can provide your "throw away" email address. Your real inbox never receives the spam.

Never open attachments unless you requested them. Sometimes, even your friends and family can have their computers infected with viruses. These viruses will often send out an email to everyone in that person's address book with an attachment, usually containing the virus. The safest thing to do is not to open attachments unless you are expecting them. You should never respond in any way to spam. Even clicking the "unsubscribe" link only verifies that your email address is valid, and you end up with even more spam. Never use your "I'm on vacation" auto-reply for the same reason; it will verify to the spammer that your email address does work. Use your spam filters instead. Some spam filters can even be set so high that you have to "white-list" anyone you want to receive email from, and everything else is sent to your junk email folder. This is especially effective because then only people you have given permission to can send you email. You should never respond to any emails asking for your name, password, or any other personal information. Often emails like this will appear to come from reliable sources, such as your bank. Remember that real companies will already have your information, and they would never send you an email requesting it.

The best thing that you can do to stop spam is to simply delete it. If everyone stopped clicking links and buying products from spam, it would no longer be profitable and would simply go away. Be a part of the solution!

Gambling

Poker isn't all fun and games.

Online poker has become a growing trend among young people today. Television shows and commercials glorifying online gambling are an every day occurrence. But there is more than meets the eye when it comes to online poker.

Something that may not be obvious is that online gambling, or any form of gambling, is illegal for young adults. Until you reach the age of majority in your state or province, online gambling is punishable by law. There is a reason for this. Gambling is a problem for many individuals in society. It can destroy lives, consuming all of your time and money. It can destroy your credit rating if you use credit cards to pay for your habit. It is important to remember that online casinos are in business to make a profit. They profit by taking in more than they pay out. Most of the time, the occasional win is offset by large losses.

Something that is becoming increasingly important is the use of credit cards for online gambling. If you use your own credit card, you could ruin your credit rating. This can make it harder or even impossible for you to buy a house, a car, or even keep you from working in some industries. If you use your parents' credit card, not only can you get grounded and punished, but using someone else's credit card is technically identity theft and fraud. It is punishable by law, and may involve serious fines, a criminal record, or even jail time. Fraud charges are outside of your parents' control, meaning they cannot choose not to "press charges". If you get caught committing fraud, even using your parents' information, you will be charged.

Online gambling can become addictive very easily. It is easy to be lured in by the promise of instant riches, only a mouse click away. You can quickly forget about the hundreds or even thousands of dollars you put into your gambling habit on your way to those so-called millions.

There are some ways to avoid the risks of online gambling. You should ignore advertisements for online gaming websites. They are not intended for you. Avoid gambling websites all together. Advertisers intentionally like to make their websites appealing to you once you arrive, practically screaming at you to take out your credit card. If you arrive at one accidentally, click away immediately. Advertisers will often attempt to lure you with offers of free money to play with. Don't fall for it! This money is only available once you make a large deposit, usually over $100.

Try to avoid sites that offer gambling without real money. Gambling of any kind creates a pattern, which is what these websites intend. Once you start gambling, it is even easier to make the transition to betting real money. Remember that gambling is illegal for minors. If you were to win anything, these websites will go to great lengths to verify your age. If you are a minor, you don't get your winnings. For young people, online gambling isn't a game of chance – it's a guaranteed loss.

The safest bet you can make online is that internet gambling will not be beneficial to you. So stay safe, and stay away. Don't bet online; you could be gambling with more than just your money.

Internet Addiction

It is not an urban myth.

Internet addiction is a growing problem among young people. With easy access to all varieties of entertainment only a click away, young people are finding it easier and easier to isolate them. Internet addiction has now become widely recognized as a disorder. Although some do not classify it as an addiction, over-use of the internet is still a cause for concern no matter who you ask.

There are more risks involved in internet addiction than you may think, many leading to permanent physical ailments. You can develop Carpal Tunnel Syndrome, a debilitating joint problem in the hands and wrists. This is caused by the posture you sit in while at your computer, and the repetitive movements involved in typing. Carpal Tunnel Syndrome can prevent you from most major types of office work in the future, limiting your career possibilities. Spending too much time on the computer can also cause dry eyes, leading to blurred vision. If you wear contacts, this can be even more serious; dry eyes can lead to bacterial infections that can potentially cause blindness.

Migraine headaches are a permanent effect of internet addiction, as many sufferers will have migraines their entire lives after the first occurrence. Backaches can develop from improper posture. This can lead to severe pain later in life, severely limiting your abilities to cope with daily living as early as your 30's and 40's. Skipping meals is common among internet addicts, and this can lead to eating disorders. Many internet addicts are overweight because of a combination of factors, primarily abnormal eating habits and lack of activity.

Lack of personal hygiene can become a problem for internet addicts, as the online world doesn't "care" if you don't shower. However, this can cause more problems than just a bad odor. If you neglect brushing your teeth, you risk causing cavities and tooth decay, as well as setting the stage for an abscess. An abscess in your mouth can cause brain damage similar to that of a serious stroke, and can even be fatal. Sleep patterns will often change for internet addicts, leading to a reduction in ability to focus during important activities such as school and work.

You should be aware of the warning signs for internet addiction. If you see yourself, your friends, or any of your family members exhibiting any of these signs, you need to speak to them or a counselor about their internet usage. Some warning signs are obvious, such as spending time online when you should be doing other things such as homework or chores, sneaking online when no one is around, and being preoccupied with getting "back online" when away from the computer. However, there are several other signs to watch out for.

Internet addicts will often lose track of time while they are online, sacrificing sleep to spend time on their computers. They may become agitated or angry when their time online is interrupted. They will often prefer spending time online rather than being with friends or family. They will disobey internet time limits set by parents, and lie about how much time they really spend online. They may become more tired or irritable than they were before the internet became a part of their life. They will often appear irritable or moody when they don't have access to the computer, but their mood will improve immediately once they log back on. They may even exhibit a completely different personality while on the computer, similar to a drug addict on a high.

Luckily, there are ways to prevent internet addiction. Play sports, go hang out with friends, or even just pick up a book. The internet is not your only source of entertainment, and is not your only social outlet. Choose other options when they are available, and only use the internet as an "extra resource" for homework assignments and the occasional email. Your social life, and your health, will benefit greatly.

If you or someone you know is experiencing an internet addiction, there is help available. Talk to your school counselors, your parents, or even your older siblings. Ironically, there are also many websites dedicated to the topic of internet addiction that may actually help. Just try to avoid becoming addicted to them.

The bottom line with internet addiction is that it is just like any other addiction. Life doesn't seem fulfilling for the addict, so they seek out a way to fill their time and their minds. The internet provides an escape for them. People can become so dependent on this escape that even without chemical dependence, which occurs in most addictions, internet addicts cannot function properly without their daily "fix". Remember that there is a whole big world out there to explore. You don't need to escape from it. If what you are doing isn't fulfilling, go find something else. There is a world of possibilities, and 99% of them are offline!

PART II

Just for Parents

Inside This Section

Just for parents

This section has been included in this book for the sole benefit of parents. While this book is targeted towards young teens and pre-teens, parents are obviously the ones who will purchase this book. You have purchased this book for the benefit of your kids, or kids you know. Perhaps you are a parent of a pre-teen who is experiencing problems on the internet. Maybe you are a teacher who wanted some material to use in class. Maybe you are a grandparent who purchased this book for your grandchildren. In any case, this section of the book is dedicated to you.

This section of the book is intended to help prepare you for the contents of the above chapters. It will help you in three key ways; First, it will help prepare you to talk with your kids about this book and why they should read it. It will prepare you for discussions you may have as a result. Second, these chapters will show you what you need to protect your children from, which is the basis of this book. Finally, these chapters will give you tips on what to watch out for in your children's behavior, and prevention & action steps you can take to protect your kids.

So, without further adieu, the following two chapters are for you.

The Hard Part

Talking to your kids about internet safety and this book.

In a perfect world, kids could go online freely. They would never have to worry about pornography, online gambling, abductions or predators. There would be no worry about the latest virus, no phishing attacks, no spyware, adware, or malware. In a perfect world, you could put a computer in your child's room for homework purposes without worrying about sexual predators taking them away. You could let your child chat with friends on the internet and know that their friends were real kids, not perverts pretending to be.

The sad fact is, we don't live in a perfect world, and every one of those things above is something to worry about. That is why it is important to talk to your kids about internet safety. There are other reasons to talk to your kids about safety as well.

First, you want to approach your kids about internet risks before they are exposed to them. Remember when you were a kid, and you did something you thought was bad? Did you run to tell your parents, hoping you wouldn't get in trouble? Of course not, you kept it to yourself. And that is what you need to prevent, by getting to your kids before the internet does. If you talk openly and honestly about the dangers on the internet, your kids will know that it is a topic you feel comfortable discussing. They will be much more likely to come and discuss it with you when they have a problem.

Second, you want your kids to know how to be aware of a bad situation long before they end up in one. This is a lot like why we tell our kids to look both ways before crossing the street. We want them to know how to avoid getting hit by a car without having to actually get hit to learn. It may feel uncomfortable now, but imagine talking to little Suzy or Johnnie after they get rescued from an online predator. THAT conversation would be uncomfortable.

You really want to talk to your kids before they get exposed to online dangers so that they know you can talk about it. There are several reasons in the mind of a child not to come running when they are in trouble. They might be afraid of getting in trouble, or losing their computer privileges. They may be embarrassed at the situation, or not want to disappoint you. They may think you will over react, ground them, punish them, or even hate them. They could even be convinced by an online predator that you cannot be trusted.

If it is so important to talk to your kids about online safety, how do you do it? It isn't easy, but there are a few ways to make the situation more comfortable for both of you. Timing of these conversations is very important. You want to do this as naturally as possible, so your kids don't think you have planned the whole conversation (even if you have). If you have more than one child, it is best to have these conversations separately to give age appropriate information to each child. Sometimes, the best place for uncomfortable conversation is in the car. It is completely private, there are no interruptions, and during the really uncomfortable parts you don't have to look your kids in the eye. Of course you should be careful and still give plenty of attention to the road.

There are some easy ways to "lead in" to the conversation. Try thinking of a topic on TV or in the movies that is related. Try something you saw in a tabloid headline after leaving the grocery store together. Or, you can just come out with it and ask if they have ever seen pornography online. Ask them if they use blogs or instant messengers. Ask them if they're on Facebook. These are all important things to know, no matter how hard they may be to ask.

The most important thing is to remember to talk with your kids, and not just to your kids. Conversation is a two-way street, which means you both have to speak. Asking probing questions, such as "how do you feel about this?" or "what do you think?" can help break the ice if they aren't willing to speak. If they are going to feel comfortable coming to you when they really need you, they need to know that you will be talking with them and not lecturing them. Lectures have a time and a place, and internet education just isn't one of them.

It is also important to let them know why you are talking to them about this, and why you care. You obviously don't want to see them hurt, so tell them that. Don't be afraid to be honest during this conversation either. If you don't know the answer to something, say so. Maybe you can figure it out together, so you can both learn new things. Remember, the more often you discuss topics like this, the easier it will become.

The topics you should cover with your kids have, in large part, been covered in this book. That is why this book will be an excellent resource for you. This book is written in such a way that, if you choose, you can read these chapters yourself first. Then, sit down with your kids and read the remaining chapters together. It will help guide you through to conversation, from why they need to know about internet safety to how they can protect their friends using their new-found knowledge.

What To Watch For

The dangers of the internet, and some warning signs

It is important for you to know what dangers there are on the internet and how to recognize when your child has become a victim. That is what this section is dedicated to. If just one parent learns how to recognize the signs of an internet crime, then one more child is safe.

Here are some general statistics about kids and the internet. Be aware, some of these are quite shocking.

- Internet use is coming earlier and earlier. An astonishing 67 percent of preschool aged children already use computers, and 23 percent of preschoolers use the internet.
- 14-17 year olds receive the highest percentage of pornographic spam.
- 94% of kids top 50 favorite websites collect personal information through the use of contests, surveys, and other forms.
- 73% of teens have signed up for a social networking site
- 27% of kids say that they would give out their real name and address in their instant messenger profile (which you don't have to give permission for someone to view.)
- 19% of kids say that they have accidentally stumbled onto a pornographic website during the last year.

- 34% of kids have been bullied, and 27% of those kids have been bullied on the internet.
- 60% of students pretend to be someone else while they're online.
- 5% of students reply to the spam they receive in an attempt to stop it.
- Spam is estimated to be worth $11 billion to the US economy every year.
- 57% of grade 4 & 5 students say they do their homework online every day. By grade 11, that number jumps to 91%.
- 35% of boys in grades 7 to 11 have purposely accessed violent or hateful content on the internet.
- 28% of kids' top 50 favorite sites contain violent or hateful content.

The statistics just continue on and on like this. It is quite startling to realize what today's kids are exposed to on a daily basis. There are ways to protect them, as will be discussed later in this chapter.

As you can see, there are a few main categories of internet crime to be aware of. Invasions of privacy, pornography, cyber bullying, online predators, spam, misinformation, violent or hateful content, gambling, and internet addiction are all things to be aware of on the internet. Your best weapon against these threats is something you already have: Knowledge.

Here are some common warning signs that your child may be a victim of an internet crime:

- Watch for secretive behavior, or spending large amounts of time on the computer. More than a few hours each day likely means that they are engaged in activities they shouldn't be.
- Unexplained phone calls or gifts from people you don't know may be a sign that your child is a victim of an online predator, as they often use these tactics on their victims.
- Your kids deleting all of the history, temporary files, etc. from the computer when they are finished using it is a sign they are viewing inappropriate websites.
- Quickly closing or minimizing windows when you enter a room often means they were viewing something you aren't meant to see.
- Strange files appearing on your computer may be viruses, spyware, adware, or malware; They could even be inappropriate photographs sent by online predators.
- Kids telling you they are going to meet friends, but not telling you who. This could be a sign that they are meeting an online friend.
- Reluctance to leave the computer can be a sign of internet addiction.
- Unwillingness to go to school or other social activities that your child is normally enthusiastic about may be a sign of cyber bullying.
- Strange charges on your credit card, or possessions going missing may be signs that your child has a problem with internet gambling.

As you can see, there are ways to spot behavioral changes in your kids that warn you of possible inappropriate content or internet crimes. But remember, you are your kids' first line of defense. You control the parental controls on the computer, you control the time they spend on the computer, and where it is located in your home. Only you can take the right steps to protect your kids.